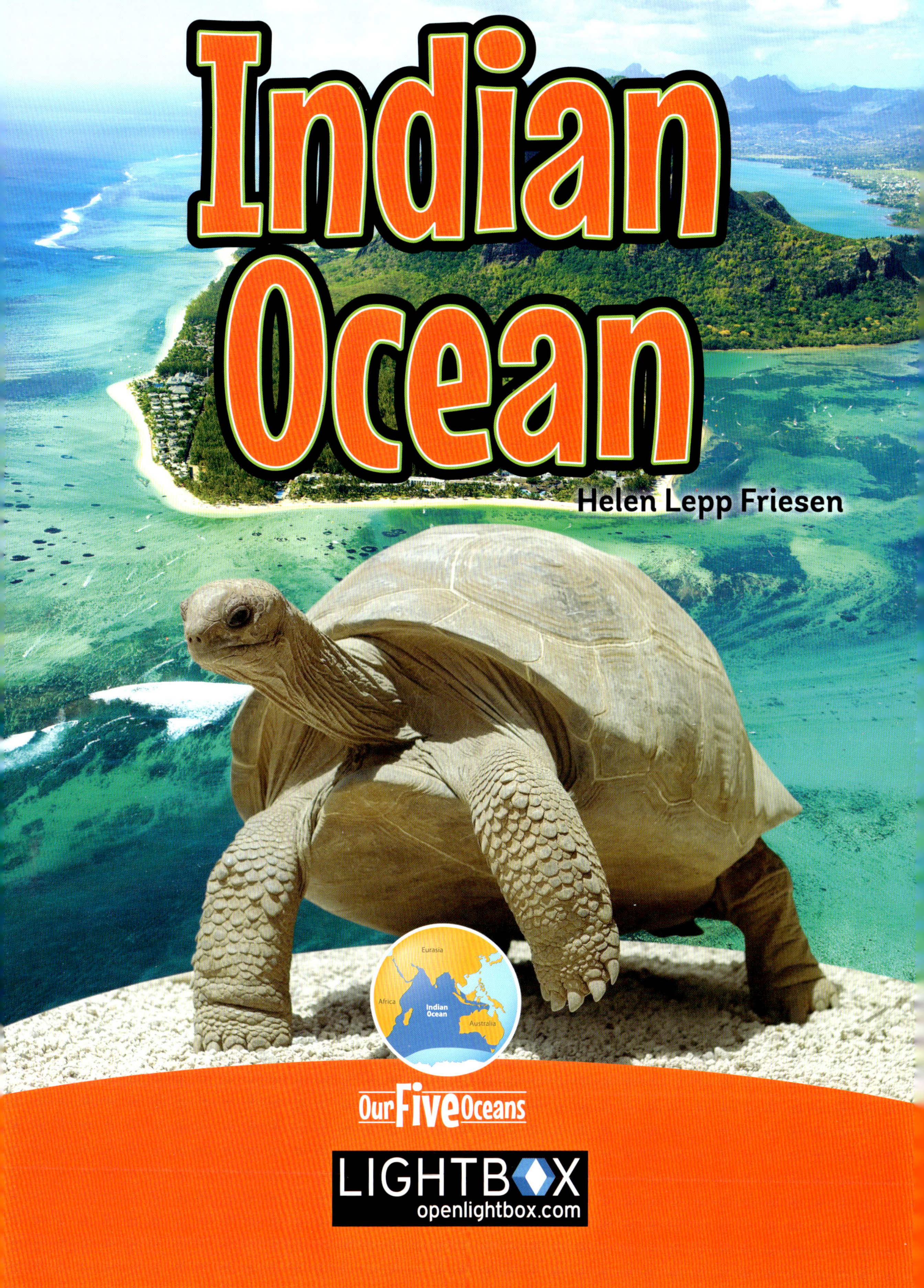
Indian Ocean
Helen Lepp Friesen
Eurasia
Africa
Indian Ocean
Australia
Our Five Oceans
LIGHTBOX
openlightbox.com

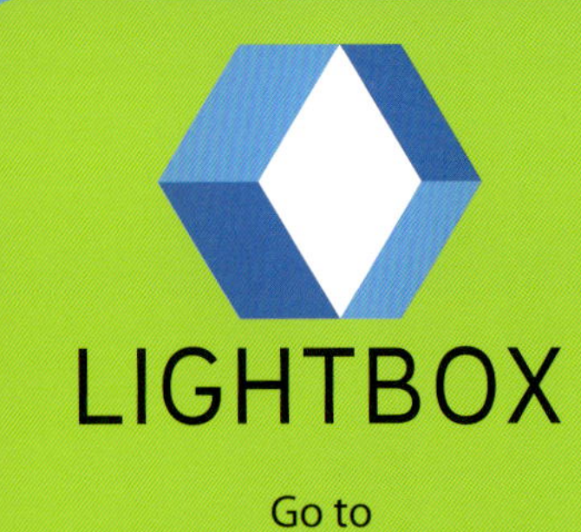


Go to
**www.openlightbox.com**
and enter this book's
unique code.

**ACCESS CODE**

**LBXN8583**

Lightbox is an all-inclusive digital solution for the teaching and learning of curriculum topics in an original, groundbreaking way. Lightbox is based on National Curriculum Standards.

## STANDARD FEATURES OF LIGHTBOX

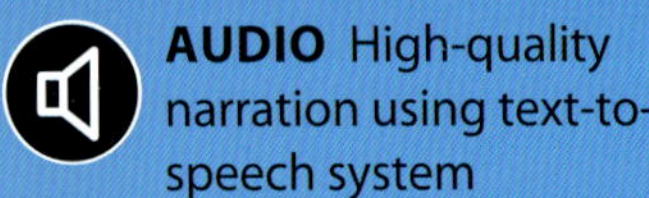

**AUDIO** High-quality narration using text-to-speech system

**ACTIVITIES** Printable PDFs that can be emailed and graded

**SLIDESHOWS** Pictorial overviews of key concepts

**VIDEOS** Embedded high-definition video clips

**WEBLINKS** Curated links to external, child-safe resources

**TRANSPARENCIES** Step-by-step layering of maps, diagrams, charts, and timelines

**INTERACTIVE MAPS** Interactive maps and aerial satellite imagery

**QUIZZES** Ten multiple choice questions that are automatically graded and emailed for teacher assessment

**KEY WORDS** Matching key concepts to their definitions

# Indian Ocean

## CONTENTS

# Global Ocean

**"When you see what goes on underwater, you realize that you've been missing the whole point of the ocean. Staying on the surface all the time is like going to the circus and staring at the outside of the tent."**

**Dave Barry, Journalist and Author**

Large bodies of water and landmasses cover planet Earth. The landmasses are called continents. Earth has seven continents, which cover 30 percent of the planet's surface. A large body of water surrounds the continents. It is called the global ocean. Basins divide the global ocean into five oceans. In order, from largest to smallest, they are the Pacific Ocean, Atlantic Ocean, Indian Ocean, Southern Ocean, and Arctic Ocean.

For many **marine** animals, from tiny corals to giant whales, the ocean is home. The ocean also supports human life. Ocean plants produce oxygen for humans to breathe, ocean plants and animals become food for humans, and ships cross the ocean to take people where they want to go.

The Indian Ocean is the ocean with the fewest partially enclosed seas. It differs from the Pacific Ocean and the Atlantic Ocean in important ways. The Indian Ocean is bordered by land to the north. Without a connection to the cold Arctic Ocean, the northern regions of the Indian Ocean are warmer.

The global ocean has a wide variety of marine animals, including about 20,000 species of fish.

# The Indian Ocean

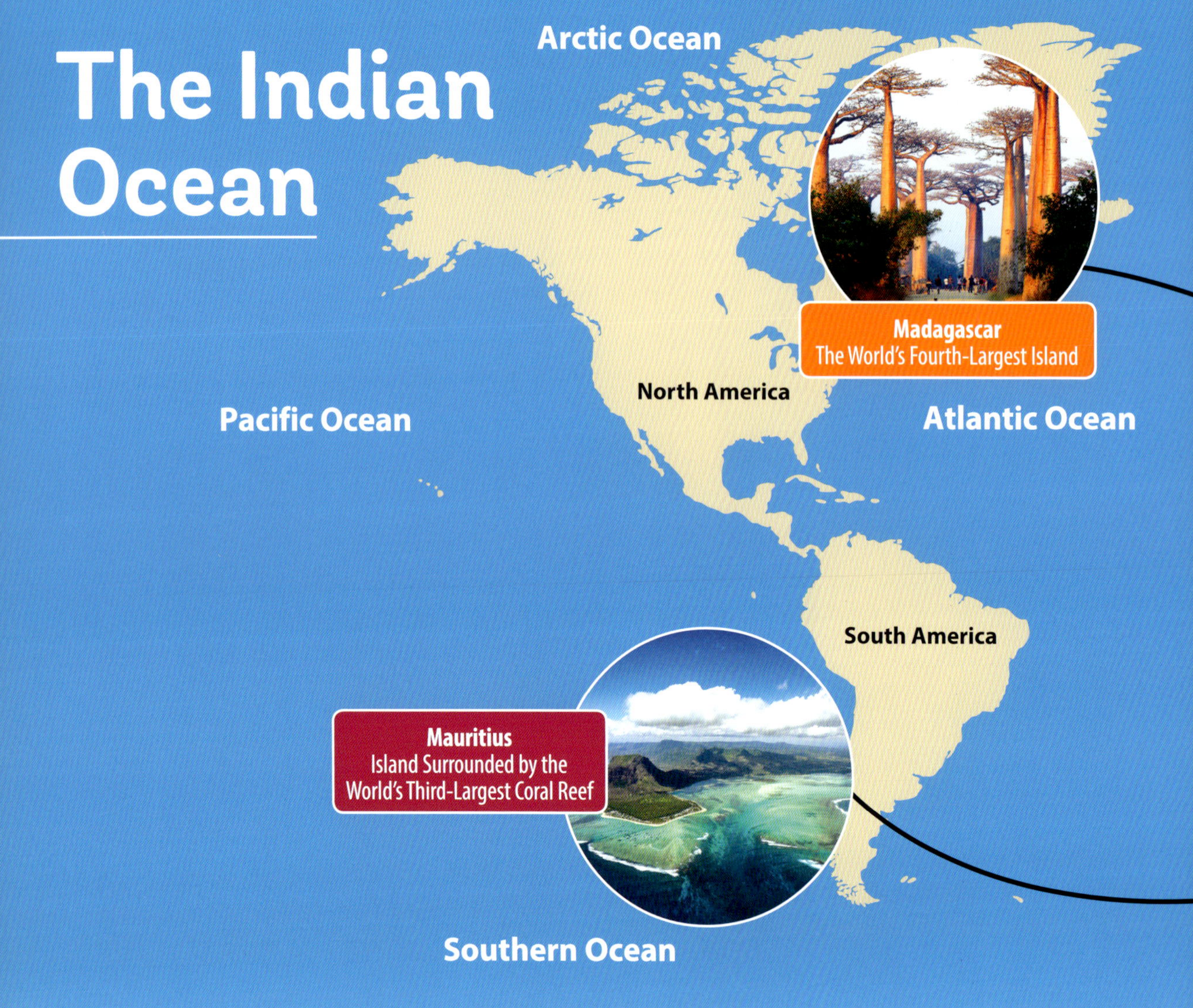


## The Warmest Ocean

The Indian Ocean is the third-largest of the world's oceans. It covers an area of approximately 28,360,000 square miles (73,440,000 square kilometers). The countries that border the Indian Ocean are India, Pakistan, Iran, and Bangladesh in the north, and Malaysia, Indonesia, and Australia in the east. In the west, the Indian Ocean is bordered by Africa and the Arabian Peninsula. The Southern Ocean borders the Indian Ocean in the south. The widest section of the Indian Ocean extends more than 6,200 miles (10,000 km).

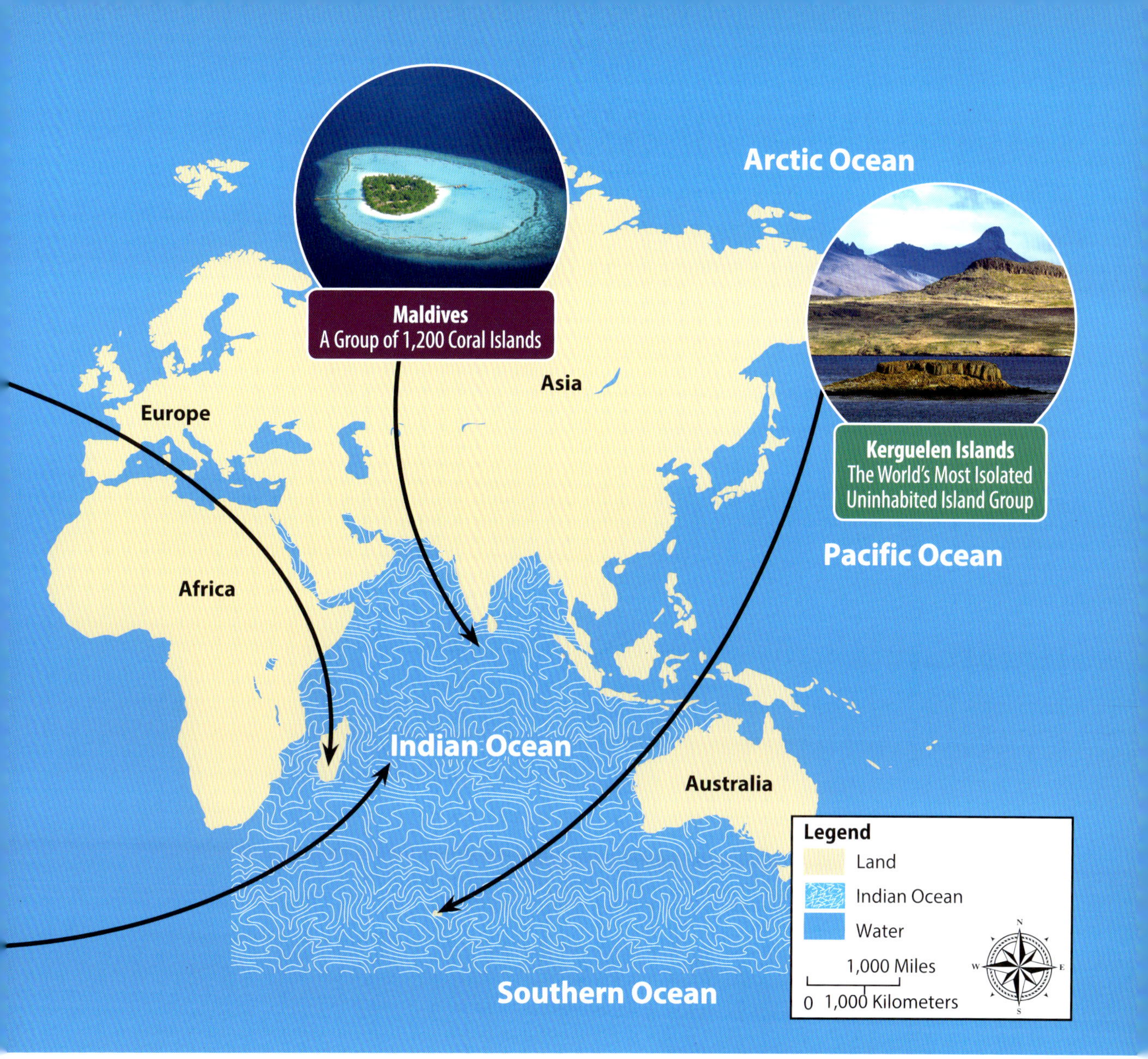

Arctic Ocean

**Maldives**
A Group of 1,200 Coral Islands

**Kerguelen Islands**
The World's Most Isolated Uninhabited Island Group

Europe

Asia

Africa

Pacific Ocean

Indian Ocean

Australia

Southern Ocean

**Legend**
Land
Indian Ocean
Water
1,000 Miles
0 1,000 Kilometers

The bottom of the Indian Ocean has its own unique geography. Ocean basins are mostly flat areas of **sediment** with some hills. There are many seamounts in the Central Indian Basin. Seamounts are inactive mountain volcanoes under the ocean's surface. Some seamounts have one or two flat tops that jut above the ocean's surface. Other seamounts rise 3,300 feet (1,000 meters) above the ocean floor.

Volcanoes formed most of the islands in the Indian Ocean.

# Indian Ocean Currents and Climate

The weather of the Indian Ocean depends on seasons, winds, locations, and temperatures. These consistent weather patterns create the Indian Ocean's climate. Changing seasons bring different weather and wind patterns. The ocean's currents also affect the climate, moving warmer or cooler water to other parts of the ocean. **Monsoons** and tornadoes are a result of the changing seasons and occur around the Indian Ocean north of the **equator**.

## Temperature

The temperature around the Indian Ocean varies, depending on the season and the location. During the southern winter months (May to October), the average air temperature ranges from 77° Fahrenheit (25° Celsius) in the **trade winds** zone to 43 to 45°F (6 to °C) in the subantarctic and Antarctic zones. For the rest of the year, the temperatures are slightly higher. During the summer, temperatures range from 77 to 82°F (20 to 22°C) in the monsoon zone to 25 to 50°F (–4 to 10°C) in the subantarctic and Arctic zones.

The Seychelles is a group of islands in the Indian Ocean. Its average temperature of 81°F (27°C) draws many tourists.

## Wind and Rain

Blustery winds cause big waves and rainstorms. From October to April, the winds are strong from the northeast. From May to October, the winds blow from the south and the west. These winds help move the ocean currents. Violent monsoons pour rain into the Arabian Sea, in the northern part of the ocean. South of the equator, the winds are usually not as potent, although the summer storms around Mauritius can be harsh.

Lagoons can create a quiet area of shelter from harsh storms.

Stressed coral can recover if the water temperature returns to normal quickly.

## Changing Climate

The Indian Ocean is home to 16 percent of the world's coral reefs. The increase in temperature due to global warming is causing shallow coral reefs to die. Scientists found that in 1998, 90 percent of the coral that was 33 to 130 feet (10 to 40 m) below the surface of the Indian Ocean died because of warm temperatures. Global temperatures are expected to continue rising. Coral is very important in the food chain. Coral reefs also provide natural protection from erosion on the shore.

## Tsunamis

The Java Trench in the Indian Ocean is the world's second-longest trench. This volcanic trench begins southwest of the island of Java and stretches more than 2,800 miles (4,500 km) north to Sumatra. It frequently experiences earthquakes. An undersea earthquake with a magnitude of 9.1 near Sumatra in 2004 caused destructive **tsunamis** that flooded coasts in Indonesia, India, Sri Lanka, Malaysia, and Thailand. Tremors reached from the Bay of Bengal to the western shore of the Indian Ocean.

Tsunamis can travel up to 500 miles (800 km) per hour. People must move quickly to high land if a tsunami is coming.

# People of the Indian Ocean

The Indian Ocean borders many different countries. Therefore, many different groups of people live on the shores of this broad, vast ocean. There is rich diversity because of the many cultural and language groups. They range from India to the East African coast, to the many islands in the Indian Ocean, Middle Eastern countries, and Australia.

## Australian Aborigines and Torres Strait Islanders

The original inhabitants of Australia are the Aborigines and Torres Strait Islanders. Skilled ocean-goers, they were sailing the ocean some 5,000 years ago. They were in Australia and Tasmania long before Europeans landed at Botany Bay in 1788. The population then was about 300,000. Although the population is now 669,000, Aborigines and Torres Strait Islanders are a small fraction of the total population of Australia. Traditionally, they were hunters and gatherers. Now, they are struggling to claim their land. Historically, about 300 different Aboriginal languages were spoken. Only about 145 languages are still spoken, including Western Desert language, Warlpiri, and Kriol.

## Swahili

Swahili people have lived on a narrow strip of Africa's east coast, from southern Somalia to northern Mozambique, for about 1,000 years. Traditionally, Swahili people have been very successful merchants. They have depended on the Indian Ocean for trade since the first century AD. Swahili people also live on Indian Ocean islands such as Zanzibar, Pate, and Lamu. Today, their population is about 500,000. Their languages are KiSwahili and English. The influences of **colonization** by the Portuguese, Middle Eastern Arabs, and the British since the 16th century have made their culture very diverse.

## Sinhalese

Sinhalese people live in Sri Lanka, an island nation in the Indian Ocean, south of India. It was first settled by people from India in the sixth century BC. Most Sinhalese people are Buddhist. About 10 percent of Sinhalese people are Muslim, while another 10 percent are Hindu, and fewer are Christian. Fishing is an important activity for coastal Sinhalese, who often fish for their livelihood. Stilt fishing is a practice that began in the last century. A stilt fisher sits on tall poles for many hours each day, waiting for schools of fish.

## The Sage's Daughter

The Hitopadesha is a collection of short stories by Brahman author Narayana Pandit. Originally written about 1,000 years ago, they offer advice and knowledge. One of these stories is "The Sage's Daughter."

A sage and his wife were unhappy that they did not have any children. One day, a kite dropped a mouse into the sage's lap. He changed the mouse into a girl and took her home to his wife.

When their daughter was 16 years old, the sage and his wife decided to find a husband for her. The father suggested the Sun God, but their daughter said, "I will burn." When the father suggested the Lord of Clouds, she said, "He is too dark, and I am afraid of thunder." The father suggested the Wind God, but she said, "He is always moving, and I am too frail." To the suggestion of the Lord of Mountains, she said, "He is too cold-hearted."

When they suggested a mouse, the daughter approved. The sage turned the girl back into a mouse. She married the mouse, and they lived happily ever after. The moral of the story is that a person's destiny cannot be changed.

# Exploration and Trade

**"We can only sense that in the deep and turbulent recesses of the sea are hidden mysteries far greater than any we have solved."**

**Rachel Carson, Environmentalist**

The Indian Ocean has a rich history of trade and exploration. Chinese silk and tea went to Europe with India's blue dye, **jute**, rice, and raw cotton. At first, the trade only went from east to west. Later, the Indian Ocean became a bustling travel route for trade going both ways. In 1612, the British East India Company defeated the Portuguese, who had maintained a **monopoly** in India and the Indian Ocean for more than 100 years. The British East India Company made an agreement with the Mughals to set up trading posts in India.

From the early 16$^{th}$ to the mid-18$^{th}$ century, the Mughals ruled most of northern India. Babur, grandson of Mongol ruler Genghis Khan, founded the Mughal dynasty. When Babur's grandson Akbar died in 1605, his empire reached from Afghanistan to the Bay of Bengal, south to Gujarat and north to Deccan. During the 17th century, the Mughal Empire began to crumble from warfare between groups and outside pressures. The British stepped into this weakened Indian state and took control.

About 1.5 million Indians make their living through commercial fishing in the Indian Ocean.

## Indian Ocean Exploration

**1820** The Indian Ocean becomes a busy route for trade between East and West.

**1837** The East India Company pioneers travel to India through the Red Sea, shortening the journey from six months to two months. Passengers and mail must cross 90 miles (145 km) of land in Egypt between the Red Sea and the Nile.

**1859** Egypt grants the French permission to dig the Suez Canal. French entrepreneur Ferdinand de Lesseps designs the 90-mile (145-km) long canal. It takes 10 years to build.

**1957 to 1958** Scientific exploration of the Indian Ocean is coordinated by many countries during the International Geophysical Year.

**1970** India becomes independent from Britain in 1947. The bustling trade routes slowly diminish in the next 20 years. The last passenger ship, the *Chusan*, leaves Bombay in February 1970.

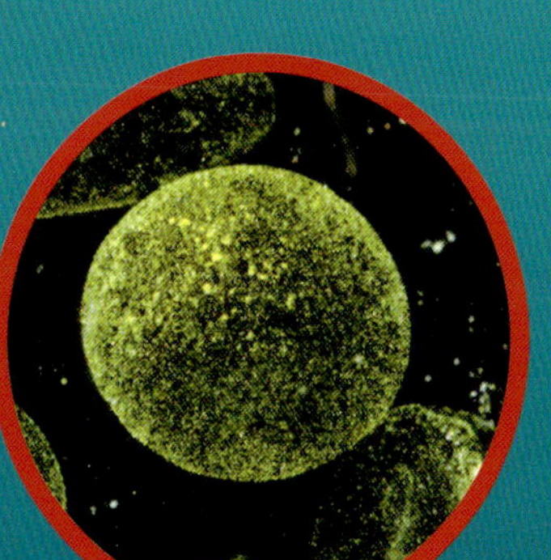

**Today** Studies warn that a rapid loss of phytoplankton threatens to turn the western Indian Ocean into an "ecological desert."

# Indian Ocean Ecosystems

An ecosystem is a group of living beings. Plants and animals make up an ecosystem. They interact with each other and with their surroundings. Within this system there are **producers** and **consumers**. Plants are producers because they use the Sun's energy. Animals are consumers. They eat what other organisms produce. This cycle of producing and consuming is called a food chain.

## Food Web

A food web diagram shows the direction that energy, in the form of food, is passed from one living thing to another. The arrows show the direction in which the energy moves.

**Loggerhead Turtles**

Loggerhead turtles and other omnivores get their energy by eating both animals and producers.

**Sea Grass**

Sea grass, a producer, gets its energy from the Sun.

**Conches**

Conches are herbivores. They get their energy by eating producers such as plants and algae.

Producers, carnivores, decomposers, herbivores, omnivores, and parasites link together to form a food chain. There are **symbiotic** relationships between the links in the food chain. These relationships can be arranged into a food web. The links in the chain are all interconnected. If one is missing, the chain is broken.

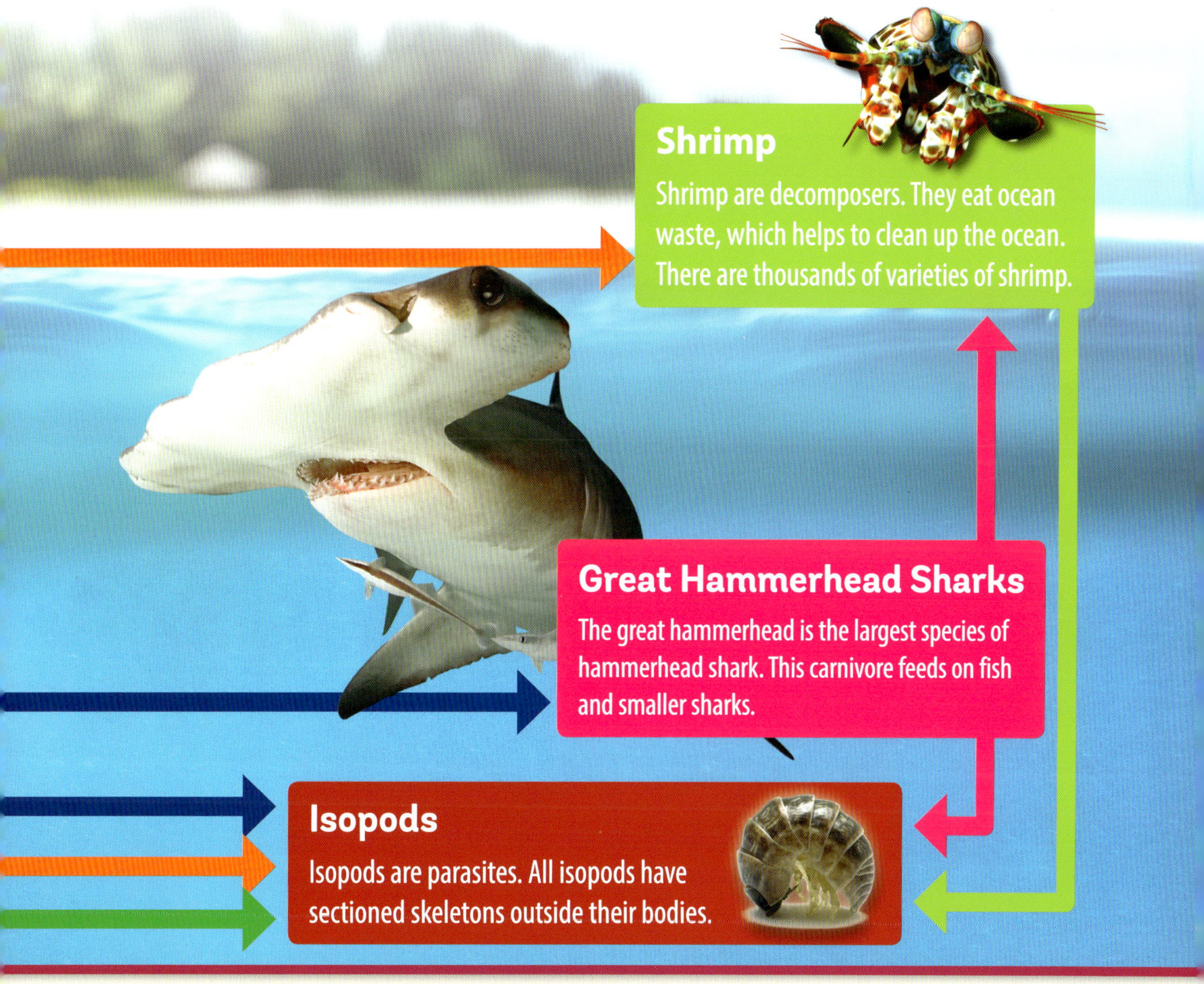

## Shrimp

Shrimp are decomposers. They eat ocean waste, which helps to clean up the ocean. There are thousands of varieties of shrimp.

## Great Hammerhead Sharks

The great hammerhead is the largest species of hammerhead shark. This carnivore feeds on fish and smaller sharks.

## Isopods

Isopods are parasites. All isopods have sectioned skeletons outside their bodies.

# Indian Ocean Life

Thousands of species of plants and animals are at home in the Indian Ocean. These species depend on the warm ocean water and climate to survive. The brilliant colors and great variety of plants and animals create a diverse marine display.

Lionfish rely on camouflage and lightning-fast reflexes to capture prey.

## Lionfish

The lionfish has white, brown, or maroon stripes around its body. It is an unusually shaped fish, with tentacles that reach out above its eyes and below its mouth. Adult lionfish can grow up to 18 inches (46 centimeters) long. They move slowly and use their fins to capture their prey. Lionfish have always lived in the Indian Ocean because the water is warm. They are nocturnal. During the day, they hide in cracks and under rocks. The sting of the lionfish can be deadly.

## Clownfish

Clownfish are also known as anemonefish. There are 30 different types of clownfish. Most are striped orange and white. They live in tropical coral reefs in the Indian and Pacific Oceans. Clownfish are omnivores. They eat both plants and animals such as algae, plankton, and mollusks. Their home in stinging anemones protects them from predators. They are not considered an endangered species. Their life span is 6 to 10 years.

Clownfish perform an elaborate dance with an anemone before taking up residence, gently touching its tentacles with different parts of their bodies until they are acclimatized to their host.

Hawksbill turtles make long migrations in order to move from feeding sites to nesting grounds, which are normally on tropical beaches.

## Hawksbill Turtles

Hawksbill turtles live in the tropical parts of the Atlantic Ocean, Pacific Ocean, and Indian Ocean. However, the Indian Ocean is important for them because of its coral reefs. Hawksbill turtles find most of their food near reefs. These turtles are omnivores. They eat algae, sponges, jellyfish, crustaceans, and fish.

## Phytoplankton

Phytoplankton is a green-tinted microscopic ocean producer that lives in the Indian Ocean and around the world. Global warming has a strongly negative effect on phytoplankton because it raises ocean temperatures out of the zone that is right for phytoplankton. This is particularly an issue in the Indian Ocean as its temperature rises drastically. The decline in the phytoplankton population affects the whole food web. Phytoplankton is the main food source for most herbivores in the Indian Ocean.

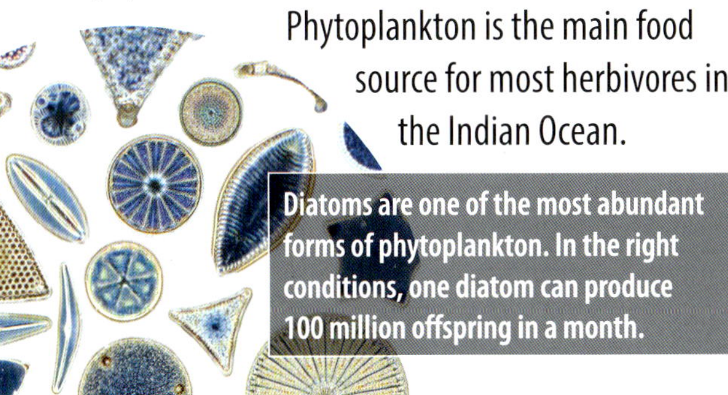

Diatoms are one of the most abundant forms of phytoplankton. In the right conditions, one diatom can produce 100 million offspring in a month.

The red mangrove grows closer to the ocean than any other tree. Its roots filter the salt out of the seawater.

## Mangroves

Mangroves grow all around the Indian Ocean. They are trees, shrubs, or ground ferns that live in saltwater marshes. Mangroves are important for a variety of reasons. They protect the coastline from tsunamis and cyclones. They also protect breeding grounds for newborn fish. People use mangrove wood as firewood, which makes it an endangered species. Coastal erosion also threatens mangroves.

# Indian Ocean Life in Danger

Many of the Indian Ocean's animals and plants are at risk of one day becoming **extinct**. People can take action to help protect Indian Ocean plants and animals. Doing research informs people about issues. Knowledge helps people make informed decisions about protecting the ecosystem.

## Write a Research Report

Learn more about why the Indian Ocean's threatened animals matter by writing a research report. Research one of the case studies provided, or choose your own Indian Ocean animal. Consider the animal both as an individual species, and as part of an ecosystem. Share your research with a partner and discuss your findings.

1. Choose a specific topic to research.
2. Decide what kinds of information you need to gather.
3. Research as much information as you can. Use multiple sources, such as books, magazines, online resources, newspapers, and experts on the subject.
4. Take notes about the facts you find in your research. Be sure to keep track of your sources so you can list them in a **bibliography** at the end of your report.
5. Create an outline for your report. Decide which facts should go in the introduction, body, and conclusion.
6. Use your notes to write a report in your own words. Try to explore multiple perspectives on the topic, where possible.
   - Your introduction should give a brief overview of your research topic.
   - Each body paragraph should deal with a separate subject, supporting your overall research topic.
   - The concluding paragraph should summarize the topics covered in the body of your paper.

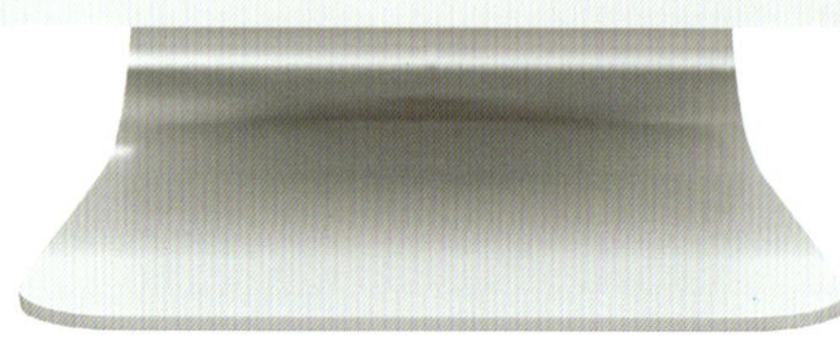

## Case Study #1

**Species:** Sperm Whale
**Status:** Vulnerable
**Population:** Estimated at 200,000 to 1 Million

Sperm whales are large animals with boxlike snouts. They can weigh up to 90,000 pounds (40,823 kilograms). The average male is 52 feet (6 m) long. Whaling decreased the sperm whale population between the mid-19th and the mid-20th centuries. About 1 million whales were hunted during that time. Now, whaling is no longer a threat, and the number of sperm whales is increasing. Today, the threats to sperm whales are pollution, getting caught in fishing nets, and consuming marine debris.

## Case Study #2

**Species:** Ploughshare Tortoise
**Status:** Critically Endangered
**Population:** Estimated at 600

The ploughshare tortoise is found only in the northwestern area of Madagascar. Ploughshare tortoises live in dry grasslands. They are small tortoises with domed brown shells, and are about 15 inches (40 cm) long. They are herbivores, and eat grass, bamboo leaves, and herbs. Wildlife traffickers are people who illegally buy and sell animals. They target rare animals such as ploughshare tortoises, which can be sold on the exotic pet market for $60,000. Another threat to ploughshare tortoises is habitat loss. Much of the land they live on is being developed into farmland.

# Changing Earth

Oceans absorb the majority of the excess heat in the air caused by global warming. The top 2,300 feet (700 m) of the oceans absorb most of this heat. Further down, the waters mix the heat more slowly.

Researchers have studied the surface temperature of oceans. Recently, they have recognized that warming is affecting fish and plant life at many depths, not just at the surface. Excess heat puts fish in danger. Most fish are cold-blooded. They need specific temperatures to survive. Fish and plankton die because they cannot tolerate warmer water.

Trees growing near the shoreline can help to protect land from some of the devastation caused by tsunamis.

The increase in water temperature has also reduced the ocean's ability to mix around the nutrients necessary for the health of marine animals and plants. A decrease in the number of phytoplankton leads to a decrease in fish populations that depend on phytoplankton as their food source. Climate change has reduced the size, age, and diversity of fish.

The rapid warming of the Indian Ocean has reduced the phytoplankton population by **20 percent** in the past 15 years.

The surface of the Indian Ocean has warmed by **2.1°F** in the past 100 years. (1.2°C)

The Indian Ocean covers approximately **20 percent** of Earth's surface.

The increase in ocean temperatures also causes coral bleaching off the coast of Sri Lanka, the Maldives, India, Kenya, Tanzania, and the Seychelles. Coral and algae have a symbiotic relationship. When the ocean's temperature warms, the algae leave the coral, which stresses and weakens the coral. It loses its color and turns white. If the algae do not return, the coral eventually dies.

## Below the Waves

The outer layer of Earth is made up of **tectonic plates** that glide over a layer of **magma** below the surface. Where the edges of the plates come into contact, there is friction. When they rub or push against each other, this friction can cause earthquakes. In December 2004, the most destructive tsunami on record occurred off the west coast of Indonesia. It started with an underwater earthquake in the Indian Ocean. At the ocean's floor, large tectonic plates moved, causing water to be pushed to the surface. This created waves 30 feet (9 m) high. The waves' height decreased while they traveled toward the coast, but they still crashed into land, causing flooding up to 1,000 feet (300 m) inland.

Earthquakes with a magnitude of 7 or greater are capable of creating tsunamis.

# Indian Ocean Uses

The vast Indian Ocean, with its warmth and beauty, attracts tourism, trade, and commerce. Traders from Arabia, Gujarat, and other coastal regions sailed the Indian Ocean in search of treasures long before Europeans. The sailors used ships called dhows with triangular sails to capture seasonal monsoon winds.

The Indian Ocean has been and still is one of the most important transit ways for the largest economies in Asia. Historically, the Silk Road connected China with the Mediterranean Sea in the trade of silk, spices, and gold. Now, China provides loans and invests in dams, power plants, ports, and railways. Major ports in the Indian Ocean include Maputo in Mozambique, Mumbai and Kolkata in mainland India, Colombo in Sri Lanka, and Port Adelaide Enfield in Australia. Shipping and shipbuilding will remain a major industry in the Indian Ocean for the foreseeable future.

Fishing is an important industry in the Indian Ocean because phytoplankton grows well there. The presence of the phytoplankton, in turn, leads to a large fish and shellfish population. Seaweed processing is a growing industry around the Indian Ocean. The large oil and gas drilling industry continues to grow.

Fishers in Kerala, India, use nets called lift nets to catch large numbers of fish and haul them out of the ocean.

# Where Do You Stand on Fishing Regulations in the Indian Ocean?

As the global demand for fish increases and other fish sources are depleted, more companies are venturing into the Indian Ocean to fish. Currently, no one organization manages the fisheries in the Indian Ocean. As fish cannot be regulated to stay in one place, it is difficult for one country to claim them. Consider the following perspectives. With whom do you agree and why?

Modern developments in fishing boats have contributed to 53 percent of the world's fisheries being fully exploited.

## For

### Environmental Agencies

"Illegal, unreported, and unregulated fishing is serious. It threatens sustainable fisheries and the health of the marine ecosystem. Laws needs to be created and applied."

### International Convention on the Law of the Sea

"Information about suspected illegal fishing can be shared among countries, making it more feasible to manage food security."

## Against

### Fishing Companies

"The ocean is huge. There is enough fish for everyone. We regulate ourselves to catch just the right amount of fish."

### Fish Markets

"Fish markets are not able to distinguish whether fish have been acquired legally or illegally. A fish does not carry a stamp of origin, so once it is caught we cannot tell where it came from."

# Issues

The Indian Ocean's ecosystem faces many threats. Climate change, growing populations, and unsound fishing practices are draining the natural resources. The decline in biological variety is affecting people and their livelihood as well as the environment. The resources of the Indian Ocean provide many goods and services. These resources need to be properly managed to protect the untouched parts of the Indian Ocean's ecosystem.

## 1 Pick an issue

Read through the issues on page 25, and choose the one that you feel is impacting the Indian Ocean the most. Develop your own point of view on this issue.

## 2 Get the facts

Once you have chosen your point of view, research the issue further. You can use sources including this book, the internet, and the library.

## 3 Use a concept web as a research tool

Read the research questions in the concept web on this page. Use the relationships between concepts to help you understand your point of view.

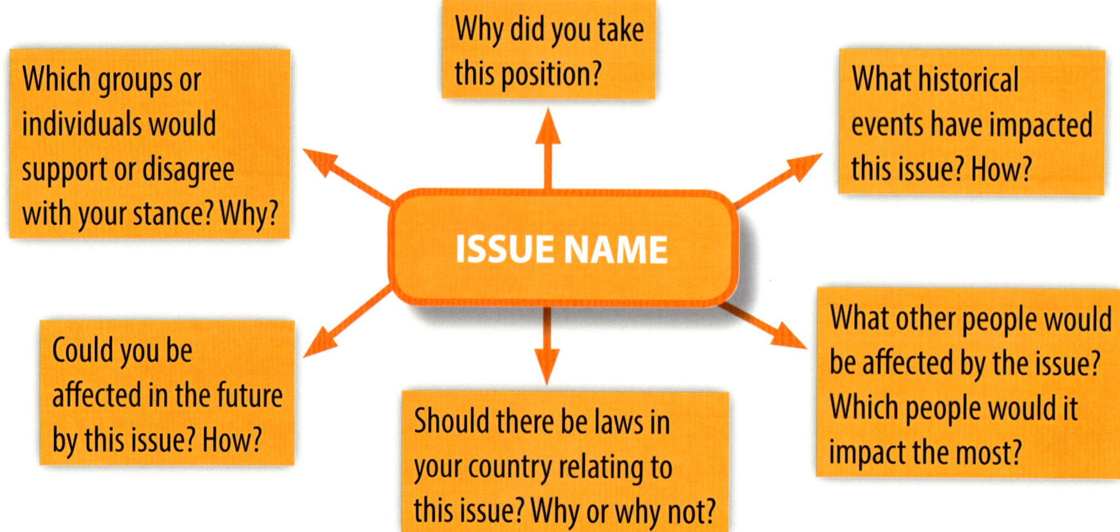

## 1 Crustacean Stocks

Crustaceans are animals with hard shells that live in water. Crabs, shrimp, krill, and barnacles are all crustaceans. Shrimp are one of the biggest fishing stocks in the Indian Ocean, but the Indian Ocean ecosystem depends upon them as well. As countries around the Indian Ocean work toward feeding their growing populations, the crustacean stocks are either fully fished or overfished.

## 2 Urbanization

As coastal centers become more urban, stress is placed on the ocean's resources. **Urbanization** and population growth put a higher demand on goods and services. This is a large reason for the decline in marine resources. With urbanization comes lifestyle changes. These can lead to problems such as water quality degradation, a decline in marine resources and biodiversity, and the destruction of vital habitats.

## 3 Extraction of Natural Resources

The Indian Ocean is home to fossil fuels such as natural gas and oil. Drilling helps the economy as it lessens a country's dependence on oil imports. However, offshore drilling has severe environmental impacts. Oil spills are a threat to the ocean's ecosystem. Drilling damages fishing grounds and contributes to climate change. Some people prefer to use renewable energy sources instead.

## 4 Environmental Pressures

The growth of urban centers adds to environmental pressures. The expectation is that by 2040, the urban population in Eastern Africa will be five times higher than in 2010. The resulting coastal development for roads, buildings, and infrastructure will impact mangroves, wetlands, and coral reefs. The increase in sewage and agricultural runoff will pollute the coastal waters of the Indian Ocean.

## 5 Destructive Fishing Practices

Destructive fishing practices deplete the fish stocks and destroy the ecosystem. Fishing with dynamite or cyanide is a major problem in the Indian Ocean. These practices kill the coral reefs on which the ecosystem depends. Recently, the Seychelles committed itself to work toward conservation, to strengthen coastal management, and to protect fisheries.

# Protecting the Indian Ocean

The Indian Ocean is in danger. Governments and other groups are making an effort to protect the animals and plants of the Indian Ocean. Researchers, scientists, activists, and citizens can all do their part in protecting the Indian Ocean. Some groups are working to protect its ecosystem.

## Our Endangered World

Founder Lindsay Meyer Karlsen came up with the idea for Our Endangered World when she returned from a trip to South Africa. There, she became aware of how many animals were being killed by poachers. She founded Our Endangered World to provide information online about endangered animals, and organizations that are doing something to protect animals and ecosystems. Our Endangered World likes to focus on the good work that conservation organizations are doing, with the hope that the conservation groups will gain more support from the wider public.

The South African fur seal population is quite strong due to the protections set in place by organizations supported by Our Endangered World.

## World Wildlife Fund

The World Wildlife Fund (WWF) works with governments, local fishers, scientists, researchers, and industry to protect the animals of the Indian Ocean. The WWF is known for working to protect animals throughout the world. It has successfully set up marine reserves in various locations across the Indian Ocean. The goal of the WWF is to safeguard and keep Madagascar's ecosystem healthy for the future, which benefits plants, animals, and people.

Olive ridley turtles are vulnerable to extinction. The WWF protects them by monitoring breeding areas and fighting climate change.

Modern fishing methods catch large amounts of fish very efficiently, but waste many fish as well. This is why Greenpeace fights destructive fishing practices.

## Greenpeace

Greenpeace is an international **nonprofit** organization that works to protect Earth and the plants and animals on it. Greenpeace has successfully fought many organizations that endangered coral reefs and marine mammals. It has also worked toward changing destructive fishing practices and promoting ocean **sanctuaries**. An ocean sanctuary is a zoned area where marine life is protected, such as a feeding or breeding ground.

## Dyer Island Conservation Trust

In 2006, Wilfred Chivell founded the Dyer Island Conservation Trust. He was concerned about a number of species, such as the African penguin, the humpback dolphin, and a wide variety of cormorants native to Dyer Island. The Dyer Island Conservation Trust conducts research with the aim of protecting the marine ecosystem and habitats at the southernmost tip of Africa. Its programs include human waste reduction along the coast. A recovery program is trying to reduce the damage done by fishing lines.

The Dyer Island Conservation Trust supports the nature reserve and bird colony, which exist to protect the animals of Dyer Island.

# Looking to the Future

**"The greatest threat to the ocean, and thus to ourselves, is ignorance. But we can do something about that."**

**Sylvia Earle, Oceanographer**

Each ocean is unique in its climate, marine life, and geography. The oceans are essential to Earth's health and need to be kept clean. More than 30 countries have coasts on the Indian Ocean. Since supplies in other waters have been used up, fishing vessels from many countries are stopping in the Indian Ocean to fish, causing problems.

Indonesia has 18 percent of the world's coral reefs, more than any other country, but they are dying at a rapid rate.

There are global groups working toward keeping the seas and oceans safe. These groups ensure and monitor the proper use of ocean resources. In 1982, the United Nations adopted the Convention on the Law of the Sea. This rule seeks to ensure that people only use the seas and oceans in a legal and safe way. With its Regional Seas Program, the United Nations Environment Program (UNEP) works to protect marine life. With its Intergovernmental Oceanographic Commission, the United Nations Educational, Scientific, and Cultural Organization (UNESCO) conducts marine research and works to manage oceans and coasts.

Green sea turtles can swim up to 35 miles per hour (56 km).

The Indian Ocean Southeast Asian (IOSEA) Marine Turtle Memorandum of Understanding is an agreement between governments that is designed to protect marine turtles and their habitats in the Indian Ocean and Southeast Asian region. Since 2000, 33 nations have signed the agreement. Partner groups are developing a network of important sites for marine turtles and working to lessen the impact of destructive fishing.

World Oceans Day was first observed on June 8, 2009. United Nations Secretary General Ban Ki-moon's message about the theme of World Oceans Day was, "Our oceans, our responsibility, emphasizes our individual and collective duty to protect the marine environment and carefully manage its resources. Safe, healthy, and productive seas and oceans are integral to human well-being, economic security, and sustainable development."

## Celebrating the Oceans

In 2015, the International Symposium on the Indian Ocean was held to celebrate the fiftieth anniversary of the International Indian Ocean Expedition (IIOE). The IIOE was one of the first multinational experiments in studying the world ocean jointly. It discovered many special characteristics of the Indian Ocean and laid the groundwork for more focused research.

Hawksbill sea turtles are endangered by habitat loss because they depend on the beaches and coral reefs that are themselves at risk.

# Quiz

1. How many oceans are there on Earth?

2. List the oceans from largest to smallest.

3. Where do Sinhalese people live?

4. What is the name of the organization that protects the marine ecosystem at the southernmost tip of Africa?

5. When was the first World Oceans Day observed?

6. What is the name of the United Nations convention that seeks to ensure that all people use the seas and oceans in a legal and safe way?

7. What role do great hammerhead sharks play in the food web?

8. How long is the Suez Canal?

9. Which island is surrounded by the world's third-largest coral reef?

10. Which critically endangered animal is found only in the northwestern area of Madagascar?

**ANSWERS**

**1.** Five **2.** Pacific, Atlantic, Indian, Southern, Arctic
**3.** Sri Lanka **4.** Dyer Island Conservation Trust
**5.** June 8, 2009 **6.** Convention on the Law of the Sea
**7.** Carnivore **8.** 90 miles (145 km) **9.** Mauritius
**10.** The ploughshare tortoise

# Key Words

**bibliography:** an appendix that lists the works referenced in a book or article

**colonization:** the act of taking control of land and people against their wishes

**consumers:** animals that feed on plants or other animals

**equator:** an imaginary line around the middle of Earth that divides it into north and south

**extinct:** a species that has died out

**jute:** a natural fiber that is used for making rope and cloth

**magma:** hot fluid beneath Earth's crust

**marine:** related to the ocean

**monopoly:** exclusive control or possession of something

**monsoons:** seasonal winds around the Indian Ocean and southern Asia that bring rain

**nonprofit:** existing for purposes other than making a profit

**producers:** plants and plantlike animals that make their own food

**sanctuaries:** places of safety

**sediment:** material, such as dirt and stones, that sink to the bottom of a body of water

**symbiotic:** a relationship in which all organisms need and benefit from each other

**tectonic plates:** sections of Earth's crust

**trade winds:** winds that blow almost constantly toward the west and toward the equator

**tsunamis:** series of large waves that strike land, caused by an underwater earthquake

**urbanization:** the process whereby people relocate from rural living to city living

# Index

## SUPPLEMENTARY RESOURCES

Click on the plus icon found in the bottom left corner of each spread to open additional teacher resources.

- Download and print the book's quizzes and activities
- Access curriculum correlations
- Explore additional web applications that enhance the Lightbox experience

# LIGHTBOX DIGITAL TITLES

## Packed full of integrated media

### VIDEOS

### INTERACTIVE MAPS

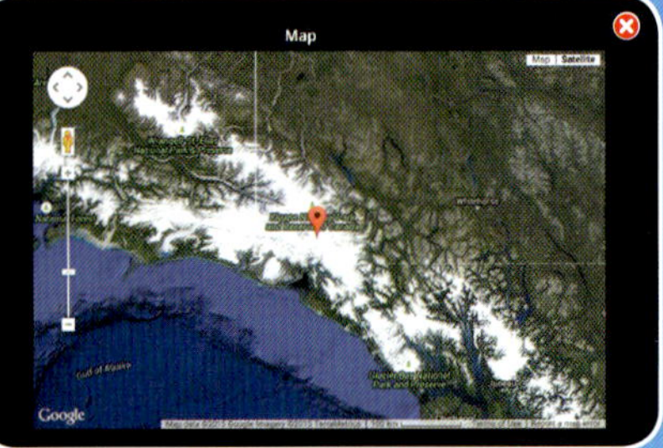


### WEBLINKS

### SLIDESHOWS

### QUIZZES

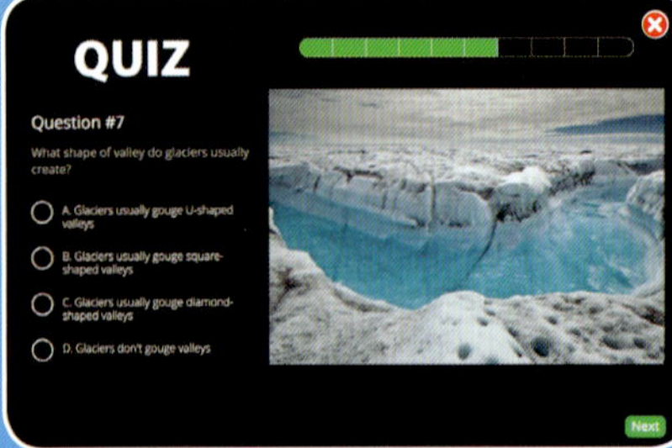


## OPTIMIZED FOR

- TABLETS
- WHITEBOARDS
- COMPUTERS
- AND MUCH MORE!


Published by Smartbook Media Inc.
350 5th Avenue, 59th Floor New York, NY 10118
Website: www.openlightbox.com





Library of Congress Control Number: 2019939920

ISBN 978-1-5105-4374-4 (hardcover)
ISBN 978-1-5105-4375-1 (multi-user eBook)

Printed in Guangzhou, China
1 2 3 4 5 6 7 8 9 0 23 22 21 20 19

052019
311018


**Photo Credits**
Every reasonable effort has been made to trace ownership and to obtain permission to reprint copyright material. The publisher would be pleased to have any errors or omissions brought to its attention so that they may be corrected in subsequent printings. The publisher acknowledges Alamy, Getty Images, iStock, and Shutterstock as its primary image suppliers for this title.


**Project Coordinator:** Heather Kissock
**Designer:** Ana María Vidal